Which Is the Tallest?

Ray Pullen

Animals are different heights.

Which of these four animals is the tallest?

A zebra grows to be about seven feet tall.
Is a zebra taller than an ostrich?

An ostrich grows to be about nine feet tall.

Is an ostrich taller than an elephant?

Lift the flap.

An ostrich is taller than a zebra.

Lift the flap.

An elephant is taller than an ostrich.

An elephant grows to be about ten feet tall.

Is an elephant taller than a giraffe?

Lift the flap.

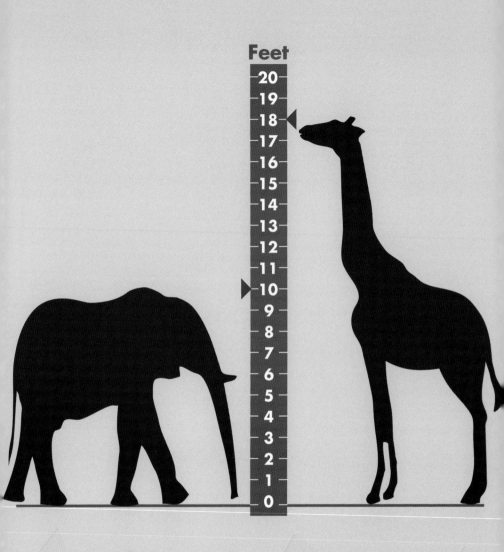

A giraffe is taller than an elephant.

giraffe grows to be about eighteen feet tall

Which animal is the tallest?

elephant   giraffe

Picture Glossary

elephant

giraffe

ostrich

zebra